" I seek your power, Lady of the Shadows
I call on your strength, Lady of three roads,
I ask your wisdom, Lady who knows,

And that this all
may now begin

I welcome you in
I welcome you in
I welcome you in "

Hedgewitch in the
Cauldron of Avalon

By

M. S. Saille

Hand bound

Copy number. *Two hundred & four A*..

ॐ *Sylvan Somethings* ☙

Published by

ℳ *Sylvan Somethings* ℬ

Glastonbury
Email: silvasix@yahoo.com

First edition
Samhain 2007

ISBN : 978 0 9557222 0 2

Introduction

Avalon

The part of Somerset close to Glastonbury has always
seemed to me to be a physical manifestation of an
out -pouring cauldron. The low- laying Levels made
up of the peat moors, full of the richness of fertility
and life transformed from death and decay,
surrounded and contained by the height and hills of
the Mendips and Quantocks, all feeding out into the
sea. It is a cauldron of both inspiration and rebirth
and maintains this feel both in spite of and because of
the work of people here. This is a man- made land,
artificially drained by the pumping stations and
rhynes and reshaped rivers that exist as a web across
it. Left to nature it would be under water at least
seasonally if not permanently in parts, and the feel of
that water is strong here. This is a Summerland.
Water plays a strong part within all Earth magic here
and it is a place of the still dark waters, perfect for
scrying and Moon magic.

This book tells the tales of walks that I have taken and
some of the magic and spells that I have woven here
and is intended to stimulate and encourage your
awareness of, and magical connections to, this land,
this earth and the natural world that we are all a part
of. For me Avalon exists on both a spiritual and a
physical level. I am one of the fortunate who is
honoured to be able to work as a hedgewitch on both.

M. S. Saille

Explore

*This book is divided into five sections,
the four seasons followed by a description of the
Cauldron of Avalon as I see it.*

*The subjects outlined within each season may
obviously be explored at any time of the year, they
are placed, however, within the time of the year that
draws me most strongly to working with them and
exploring them further ~ we are all still learning, and
may we continue to do so throughout our lives.*

*But the ways of magic are flexible to need and
therefore when I need to act, for example to make a
charm or token, I will do so,
no matter the season.*

*All of the ways of weaving magic included within
this book are intended to help and to heal and
therefore to be used when the need arises and when
your intent is true, a clear mind, a clear and positive
intent and an awareness of the repercussions of your
actions are what is needed.*

May your wishes be wise ones.

~ Merry Meet~

Contents

A Spring Walk...

The droves are bordered with the life of
the season, I know these leafy trees well,
Alder and Birch and Willow dominate
with specimens of others obvious in their
non-conformity. Pockets of Thorn,
Elder, bright in bloom, the occasional
Oak and Apple all of these are
acknowledged as old friends along this
path I tread.
The droves crisscross the levels and
ditches and waterways are bridged with
both modern and older crossings.

I stand on a familiar crossing of old
stone and as water flows below me, air
sweeps past and fire flashes as lightning
in the sky.
The raw elements surround me and I
experience the energy swirling
weaving it into the charm,
that rests in my palm...

Charms and Tokens

Making a charm from what you find as you walk is
an intuitive and seasonal magic..

Right from the beginning however I was taught that
you never perform magic for another without both
their knowledge and their permission.

It is wrong to influence the path of another without
their knowing consent.

Like the ripples on a pond when a pebble is thrown
into it the impact of your actions will radiate out and
away from you and then will bounce back.
So…

Before any magic
Be sure you have thought through any repercussions
Work honestly and openly

And with full permission

Be sure your intention is clear,
And good
And true

Merry Meet & Merry Part
& Merry Meet Again….

Charms can be made of leaves, grasses, twigs, bark or
that little piece of sheep's wool caught on the barbed
wire. I bind appropriate leaves with a strand of ivy, or
inscribe a word or initial on a leaf.
These charms carry the intent that you place in them
with their making, as well as the charge or energy of
your spirit that you can add. They may be cast into a
stream to carry something away or to clear energy.
They may be placed on, or tied to, an appropriate tree
to hold or earth a wish or spell. Either of these two is
appropriate as these charms and tokens are made
with what is already found in the area and as such
will not be seen as an eyesore or rubbish.
They are natural, as Hedgewitchery is natural.

☽○☾

These small gatherings of natural materials may be as
simple or complex as you wish. If not cast away or
hidden to release the energy, they may be given or
kept as tokens to be carried or hung up over window
or door or placed as a wish on an altar.
These small things may be as simple as a single seed
or nut or stone, they may be a tied bunch of flowers, a
twist of herbs or a knotted piece of grass or even a
rhyme written on a piece of bark.

Walking along side rivers and streams, remember
that shells may be gathered as representations of the
element of Water, or as a container for a small charm.
As I have walked along the River Brue I have
gathered shells left by the Heron, the Fisher King.

A pebble or chip of stone that catches your eye may be used for the element of Earth, or a crystal or that sprinkle of sand or dry earth.

Feathers found can be a symbol of Air, or of a particular Goddess or God, for example swans are frequent visitors to this area and I have used their white feathers as representations of Brigid.

For Fire I call on the fire of my spirit or of the lightning struck tree or lightning itself as it illuminates the sky, or the fiery heat of the Sun, life giver.

Plants and herbs carry meanings and magic ~ for example blackberry, cat tails, nettle and clover, each can represent, can be a symbol, can lend their energy to yours as you include them in your posy, your charm, your token, your spell.

Trees also carry many meanings that can be woven into a charm. Twigs can be bound in twos or threes with grasses or bindweed or whatever is to hand to create a combination of meanings or a balancing of male and female. For example, Oak for male and willow for female in creating a token for a couple could well be appropriate, however Willow may also be used singularly to represent water or experience, lessons from adversity, and Oak to represent strength and protection.

Follow the meanings you know and learn from your contact with the trees themselves. Some of the simple correspondences for trees that I work with locally are shown on pages 16 ~ 21 and may be used as a starting point.

Research that tree on the hill, or those that line the
road you often walk down, or fill your nearby park.
Ground yourself in your local environment, no matter
how wild or industrialized or urban.

Open yourself to the meaning, the particular 'feel' of
types of trees, listen, really listen and you will be able
to sense how different they all feel, and weave those
differences into your charms and tokens.
If you live in an area where you do not feel safe
exploring a woods alone, or sitting under that tree in
the park or local waste land then take a friend who
doesn't mind spending a while watching over you, or
experiencing the place with you.
I had a large dog as my companion, who got very
used to spending time just sitting in odd locations!
All of the following is not always possible in all
locations, so adapt!!

The idea is to get as close to the Earth as possible, to
break down the dichotomy of 'us' and 'nature' ~ there
is no real separation. We need to remember, to relearn
the web of connectedness between all things.

To Feel

*You find the tree that attracts you, and stand
before it.
Take off boots or shoes and touch the Earth with
your feet,
Wriggle your toes; is it warm, cold, soft or hard?*

*Allow your senses to experience fully without
judgement.*

*Breathe deep
Slow down*

*Imagine growing roots down into the Earth,
root yourself in its stillness.*

*Reach out your hands and touch the tree, just
gently, lightly, barely touch.
How does it feel?
rough/ smooth, warm / cold, velvet/ sticky
Just experience the sensation, let it wash through
you.*

*Breath deep
Slow down
And open all your senses*

*Be open to touch, to sound, to scent,
to everything…*

Press your hands more firmly against the tree
Lean your forehead against it
Rest there
Breathe deep
Slow down
And feel…
Try to have only the tree in your consciousness
Acknowledge nothing else
Take the time
Slow down
Breathe.

Take as long as you need, then reverse.
Slowly
Remove your forehead from the tree,
Slowly
Remove your hands
Slowly
Step back.
Note what you experienced, note what you
sensed.
Say thank you!

Sometimes it may feel more appropriate to simply
sit down and lean back against the tree,
Or to climb up it
However seems best to you, just take the time…
And discover.

All of these experiences will add to your knowledge of the trees, and will aid you in deciding what to add to your charms and tokens.

Practical experiences enhance your book learning.

Discover your local mineralogy; are there crystals or Hag stones? [Pieces of flint with natural holes through them] where you live? All that you find may be incorporated into your magic.

This area is one of peat, all of life from death, rebirth and regeneration. This is contained and supported by an under layer of clay.

However the hills that surround have local potato stone, a red and cream agate. Explore the geology of where you live; it is a sometimes hidden and often ignored or unrecognised layering of landscape that creates a '*feel*' to a place.

Some of the early walks of my magical youth were in a decaying industrial landscape being reclaimed by nature.

The scrub trees of Hawthorn and Elder, following the invasive, ever present, ever green Ivy became well-known companions on my magical path as I bound charm and token for myself and others.

May blossom was twisted with Blackthorn into a crown for Beltaine to welcome in the fertility of Spring, Elder used for creativity, regeneration and to ward off evil with a feather used for clear thought and communication and nettles to banish fear...

Today I walk in a less industrialised landscape that supports a greater variety of wildlife, but the principles remain the same.

A Simple Love Spell

Thinking of a friend who has asked for help I set out on my walk toward the bridge.
I have chosen mid- morning and a path that should lead past appropriate trees.
I gather long grasses and a leaf off the apple tree to use as a parchment
~ I inscribe her initials onto the back of the leaf with a twig from the tree ~
wrap the grasses round both to bind, and knot it using a knotting rhyme to charge.
As I walk May blossom catches my eye so I pick a sprig and twine it into the charm with a kiss. I reach the bridge.
I use the water to symbolise emotion to carry the charm and release the magic,
I wish her well, I breathe in the feel and energy of the land all around me,
I wish her an open and honest heart
I visualise her happy, fire of my spirit
And I release the charm
Dropping it into the water.
I breathe out, releasing all...

Trees

Some Simple Meanings of Local Trees

Alder ~

This tree stands tall along the lanes and in hedgerows, often with catkins and cones both present, which to me seems to symbolize male & female in balance.

Common in marshy and swampy land, it is the tree that slowly helps to transform such places into firmer more solid land. It is generally viewed as a masculine water tree and traditionally used to protect against drowning. It is also connected with death, resurrection, integration and slow transformation.

I weave it into charms and tokens mainly for this representation of transformation, but also to aid with the integration and acceptance of change.

[Latin name: **alnus glutinosa***]*

Apple ~

Avalon is full of apple orchards blessing us all with fruit of love and magic, healing and immortality. Found in orchards young and old, and free amongst the hedgerows, this tree scents the air with intoxicating richness. To me it represents the Triple Goddess, the Maiden when in full bloom, the Mother ripening once blooms are shed and the Crone when covered in the ripe sacred fruit.

The apple is a symbol of love and magic, cut in half crossways it reveals the pentagram and is the fruit of immortality.

The Apple tree is a connection between this realm and the realms of the otherworld, a gateway into the world of magic, it is the epitome of Avalon.

[Latin name: **malus , domestica** *or* **sylvestris***]*

Beech ~

With its smooth trunk and golden leaves from Autumn through Winter into Spring, Beech is an easy tree to spot. Common to woodland and less so on the levels, I seek it out for charms of learning and wisdom, old objects, old learning. Beech is also seen as a healing tree.

[*Latin name:* **fagus sylvatica**]

Blackthorn ~

The white blossom of this thorn herald the Spring and the bitter sloe gives plenty of itself in Autumn.

Note well its location in the Spring when the whiteness makes it most noticeable. Blackthorn is in blossom before it is in leaf and its flowers are a sharp white in contrast to the creamier hawthorn bloom that it precedes. The Blackthorn is a masculine tree used for divination and wish magic as well a protection.

So if your thoughts are full of wishes weave in a little of this tree, leaf or thorn or bloom or fruit as is appropriate to your wish.

[*Latin name:* **pruns spinosa**]

Elder ~

Almost as common as willow, due to its similar property of growing from any small twig that is planted, this gift of a tree bears creamy white blooms in Spring and its dark purple fruit in Autumn mark it most obvious at these seasons.

It is known for creativity, is a feminine tree, and is often thought to represent the wisdom of the Crone.

I follow tradition and use it to keep evil away, placing a piece of elder for protection in a charm. Use a small piece of a hollow twig roughly shaped into a whistle or a flute as elder flutes were thought to be used to summon spirits to protect.

The flowers are for freshness and new beginnings. I use both the flowers and fruits in my kitchen as well as in charms. It is a versatile magical tree.

[Latin name: sambucus nigra]

Hawthorn~

Also called Tree of the May or May Tree, its bright red Haws are used in rights of fertility and happiness. In Avalon we have the Holy Thorn [crataegus monogyna praecox] which flowers in winter and May, so this tree seems to be ever visible within the hedgerows here with flowers ranging from creamy white to deepest pink.

May flowers or May leaves for the May Queen, signal youth and fertility and all the potential that youth contains. I use the blossom in charms to usher in love but also to represent the Maiden aspect of the Triple Goddess. This tree can also be representative of the need to consider and accept change.

Treat this tree with respect as tradition dictates that misfortune will fall on those who cut it down. Ask before you gather, and exchange a token before you leave.

[Latin name: crataegus monogyna]

Hazel ~

A hedgerow tree, I have also found many old coppices gone to wild with hazel nuts a plenty. This is a tree of wisdom and inspiration, protection and water divining and is one of the trees which border the realms of magic. It is Brigid's tree.

Hazel nuts are traditionally thought to contain all wisdom. I use nuts or twigs when seeking new understanding of a situation or as a symbol of questing.

Hazel twigs are flexible and twisty especially those from a coppiced tree, they lend themselves as the basis of circlets or crowns for those undertaking an initiation. I have used them to twist into a bangle to lend focus during a meditation.

[*Latin name*: corylus avellana]

Oak ~

These stand old and tall and proud in woodland and on the edges of the cauldron. Sometimes they appear on the edges of the rhynes alone or in small groups near gateways or in the older hedgerows.

Oak is traditionally used to represent masculinity, strength, wisdom and protection, it can attract both energy and illumination.

Sessile Oak [quercus petraea] has leaves with stalks but no stalks on acorns. Common Oak [quercus robur] vice versa.

The Oak King rules the summer half of the year, bringing fertility with strength that is also nurturing. This may often be seen by the manner in which this tree supports a huge variety of other life within its branches.

Lean back against the sturdyness of its trunk and breathe in the calm support that it offers.

Sprigs of young oak leaves can represent the male youthfulness, acorns its guardianship, masculine protection and potential.

It is the Druid's tree.

Silver Birch ~

An elegant and straight hedgerow tree on the edge of marshland, with a bark that peels in curls off the tree, it is very useful as a natural paper substitute for spells and tokens.

Use this tree itself as a symbol for protection, new beginnings, wisdom and purification. A curl of its bark or a small bundle of the appropriate number of twigs may be included in a charm or token.

[*Latin name*: betula pendula]

Willow ~

This area is known for its willow, both pollarded and coppiced. It often lines the banks of the rivers and rhynes. Willow may be used to represent femininity, water and experience through adversity. Because of its flexibility it can be used to weave things together. Traditionally used in basket making, this property is also useful when making crowns and charms. A circlet woven from willow may then have other things woven into it, freshly picked appropriate herbs for example, or ivy and hawthorn for a maiden's crown...

Willow appears in myriad varieties on the levels, including:

Crack Willow,[salix fragilis]
Goat Willow,[salix caprea]
Weeping Willow [salix x sepulcralis]
White Willow[salix alba]
Osier [salix viminalis]
Red Willow [salix alba britensis]

The different colours of these varieties can be used to bring in a little colour magic when weaving charms.

The gnarled shapes of the trunks of old pollarded willow may have cavities suitable for the placing of charms, wishes or tokens. They may be twisted or have holes passing all the way through them, perfect for natural window magic or visualisations or use as gateways.

The willow is a very flexible and versatile tree, I feel lucky that it is abundant in this area. However the first willow tree I truly noticed and appreciated was a huge ornamental weeping willow in someone's garden near to where I grew up, its draped fronds always fascinated me and were great for twisting into shapes even then.

Yew ~

A tree of transformation, of death and rebirth, its power may enhance your natural magical abilities and it holds all the ancient wisdom.

It is the old one, the wise one, the all-knowing one. There is a small group of Yew trees I know very well and one in particular that just calls me to climb up, and I often do (no matter how unsuitably dressed!) and just sit and calm and centre, just being open to any messages that it might send, or focusing on a particular transition or transformation.

Use yew with care as it is toxic. Berries and bark, twigs and sprigs may be used for charms of transformation, or for those of endings.

[Latin name: **taxus baccata**]

Plants

*Some magical meanings of a few of the plants
that may be found around the levels*

Artemisia ~

*Mugwort, Lads Love, Wormwood are all varieties of
Artemisia, named for Diana Artemis. All of them have
Otherworldly connections:*
*Lads love is said to aid the dead to sleep, but also for magic
to aid male fertility!*
*Mugwort is used for amulets, and charms to protect
against magic and to encourage dreams of awareness and
fortelling.*
*Wormwood is also said to help the dead to sleep and has
strong connections with the Otherworld and the fey.*

Blackberry / Brambles ~

*This is a plant of thorny protection, it guards well all that
it surrounds.*
*I gather its leaves for protective charms and its fruits for
syrups and jams. Wreaths of the brambles are easily made
to hang as symbols of protection around garden or home.*

Broom ~

*Use broom as your broom for sweeping a ceremonial circle,
it is good at clearing. It should always be gathered with
respect [as with any plant or item that will be used for a
magical purpose] and a fair exchange made for what you
gather. It is a plant that encourages good fortune.*

Burdock ~

Used in charms and tokens of protection.

Cat tails ~

Cat tails, reeds and rushes represent the wind to me and may be woven or plaited into many shapes for poppets, charms or tokens. Folk lore tells not to weave rushes into a ring for looking through or you will see the fairy folk and then be blinded.

Chickweed ~

For gentle Moon magic and animal magic, especially birds.

Clover ~

A plant of consecration, of pentacles and other ceremonial tools, the trefoil is strongly of the element of Earth. I use it in protective charms and generally to bless.

Comfrey ~

This plant is one I use in charms for safe travel and charms to bring a traveller home again, and of course in healing magic.

Cowslip ~

Sacred to Freya, to the Mother and to Love Goddesses and useful in charms connected to love as it also has the Mother's protective nature. Because they seem to be getting so rare nowadays please do not pick from the wild. I honour them and gather only fallen blooms when I see them.

Daisy ~

A protective plant of the fairies, and one which I was taught is appropriate for baby blessings and namings.

Dandelion ~

Said to be connected to Hekate and the element of air. The seed heads will carry wishes. When we saw them on the breeze my daughter would call them fairy wishes.
It is the root that pierces deep into the Earth and connects to the Otherworld and immortality.
Most gardeners will thank you for digging up the root to use it thus!

Fern ~

For charms to pass unseen, or rather to not be noticed it is traditional to use fern, bracken, seed gathered at Mid Summer's eve. Other ferns have links with male fertility rites, especially the roots.

Feverfew ~

This may be used magically in charms to protect against accidents and against sickness.

Ivy~

To bind, to bless, to secure and appropriate woven as wreathes to wear at any celebration or decorate any sacred space. Generally seen as feminine, ivy also has male connections as the nest of Saturn's bird the wren. Ever present, ever green, ever growing, full of life, the ivy.

Marsh Marigold ~

Of the Earth Mother, of nature, of strength within femininity. Traditionally used in garlands at May Day.

Meadow Sweet ~

For love, for the Maiden, for the bride and to invoke Bloddeuwedd.

Nettle ~

Use this plant in charms to banish fears ~ carefully gathered! [And young nettle tops also make marvellous soup.]

Old Mans Beard ~

Twine into charms for renewal and survival and for endurance.

Wild Rose ~

Pale pink and five petaled use for charms and tokens to invoke love and joy and the Triple Goddess.

Yellow Iris ~

Charms for purification.

Poppets

Dolls, Wishes and Representations

*This year's Brigid doll,
an Imbolc poppet*

A standard poppet is a representation of a person, a
simple doll that can be used as a focus for your magic.
It is a symbol.

An Imbolc Poppet

Each year I make a doll of Spring, a Brigid doll.
I take a walk out on the Levels,
usually somewhere I have not been in a while or
a path I have not walked at all.
I create the poppet as I go using what I find as I walk,
some years these have been mainly based around
reeds, other times twigs and grasses.
Each is unique and incorporates the energy of that
Winter passing and that Spring arriving.

One walk to make it, the next day I keep it with me to
charge it, then I formally welcome it into my home,
welcoming the potential of the year to come
and the energy of Brigid,
Goddess of hearth and home, into my home.
Then she is put to bed,
under tree or under hill or in a stone circle
My annual ritual.

Poppets are not a simple tool and they take time and concentration in the making, however they can be very effective.

I would suggest doing most work with poppets in a circle because it reinforces the clarity and focus that is needed. Cast your circle in the usual way of the tradition that you follow or you could use the solo circle method outlined on pages 41~ 42.

Try to work with the appropriate phase of the moon, for example:
The waxing moon to use the growing energy up to a full moon would be best to give strength and draw in healing.
The waning moon would be best to use the energy down to a dark moon to clear away sickness or banish infection.

The standard poppet used for healing, protection or love magic, is a shape cut from natural fabric, stitched around with cotton, and stuffed with a mix of appropriate dried herbs and flowers.
However poppets can also be created out of appropriate twigs, plants and herbs gathered from your garden or places that you walk or visit. These gleanings are then twisted and tied and formed into the rough shape of a person, male or female. This is the method that I use most often.
Other common methods of poppet making involve moulding a figure from clay or wax or as I mentioned in The Kitchen Cauldron, out of bread dough.

A charm or rhyme is then created to bless and activate the poppet which is consecrated with the four elements as you say your charm.
You may consecrate in any manner that you are familiar with according to your own path or tradition. To me consecration by the elements seems the most appropriate and is clear and simple to achieve:
To consecrate with Air and Fire pass the poppet through the smoke of appropriate incense.
To consecrate with Earth and Water sprinkle lightly with salt water.

> *Poppet, Poppet ~ Made by me,*
> *Poppet, Poppet ~ You I see,*
> *Poppet, Poppet ~ Charmed and blessed,*
> *Poppet, Poppet ~ Do your best,*

> *Poppet, Poppet ~*
> *Carry true*
> *All the energy*
> *I charge to you*

The creation of the poppet is a physical task which helps to focus your energy into the charging and empowering of it, aided by the appropriate symbology of the materials that you are using.

> *Poppet, Poppet ~*
> *Carry true*
> *All the energy*
> *I charge to you*

The poppet may be charged in the same way that you would charge any item.

For example, one way to charge a poppet would be to call upon the element most appropriate for the work you intend the poppet to do [see 'touching the elements'] and, holding the poppet in your hands (or using a wand or athame to direct the energy toward the poppet), draw on and visualise the energy of that element flowing into the poppet to charge it.

Another way to charge a poppet would be to use the energy of the Moon to empower it by placing the poppet within the light of the moon and visualizing the moonlight infusing it . [see page 78]

> *Poppet, Poppet ~*
> *Carry true*
> *All the energy*
> *I charge to you*

The hardest part of the task is the next stage manifesting the link between the poppet and the person for whom it is being created.
I forge this link through visualisation and the use of a rhyme or chant.
My most common visualisation for a healing poppet being that of two circles, person in one, poppet in the other, and I slowly view them as moving to overlap and then superimpose one on top of the other.
I use actions to reinforce the visualisation.

In my left hand, palm up, I place the poppet and say/chant

"Be in a circle, I am healing you"

I see the poppet within a shining sphere of light.

In my right hand, palm up, I place a token to represent the person I am working for (a picture, or their name written on a piece of parchment for example) and say/chant

"Be in a circle, you are Healing too"

I see the person within a shining sphere of light.

I then move my hands together until they are just touching side by side. I see the two spheres overlapping and say/chant

"Unite ~ be as one"

I then fold my left hand onto my right, linking the two hands together, linking the healing energy of the poppet to the person. I see the two spheres merge into one and say/chant

"Unite ~ be as one"

I generally repeat this whole sequence three times until I am secure in the feeling that the link is forged.

Others utilize different visualisations to build a link between poppet and person. For example: the forging of a chain or the growing length of a silver cord linking the two. There is no fixed rule, practise and see which best works for you!

However it is this link, created between poppet and person, that is at the heart of the magic of poppets.

Left Hand ~
Holding poppet

Right Hand ~
*Holding image or token
of person being healed.*

**Be in a circle,
I am healing
you**

**Be in a circle,
you are
healing too**

*Move hands together to touch
and slightly overlap*

Unite ~ Be as one

*Close hands together
palm to palm forging
the link between
poppet &
person.*

**Unite ~ Be
as one**

*Repeat these
words and
actions thrice.*

The poppet may be given to the person for whom it was created, for them to have a visual reminder of the healing, or it may be kept on your altar for a moon cycle. At the end of this time the magic fades and the poppet may be laid to rest,

Hold the poppet in your hand, or if you have given it to the person for whom it was created focus and visualise it laying in your hand and say:

> *Poppet, Poppet ~ Made by me,*
> *Poppet, Poppet ~ you I see,*
> *Poppet, Poppet ~ Charmed and blessed,*
> *Poppet, Poppet ~ Now at rest,*
> *At rest,*
> *At rest.*

I then take it all apart and scatter or bury the pieces, returning the energy to the land. If you have given the poppet to the person for whom you created then it is up to them whether they keep it or whether they take it apart and scatter the pieces, the charge has been laid to rest and the poppet is empty. Generally if I am asked by the person concerned, I suggest taking it apart as that creates a feeling of closure.

The Pattern for a Sewn Poppet

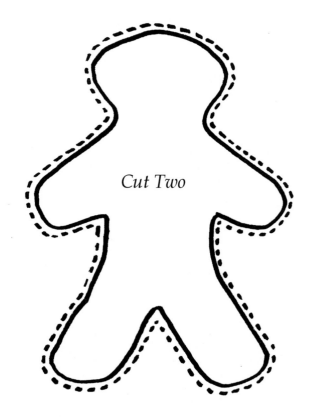

Cut Two

Trace the pattern round onto a fresh piece of paper, cut it out and pin it to your fabric. Then cut around again creating two identical fabric shapes.

A Sewn Poppet for Healing

Firstly remember to have the permission of the person
you are performing the healing magic for.
For healing
I would use either a natural skin- coloured fabric for
a physical healing, or for emotional healing I would
more likely choose a mauve or purple fabric.
For the stitching I would use a cotton or wool of the
same colour.
If the person has a particular association with one
fabric or colour then that can be used, however
whenever possible try to stick with natural fabrics.

Some of the herbs and plants with strong associations
to general magical healing are:
Blackberry
Chicory
Comfrey
Lavender
Lily of the Valley
Mint
Mustard
Nettles
Peony
Sage
Verbena
Willow
Wood Betony

I would include one or more of these to fill the poppet
and sometimes it may also feel appropriate
to add a small crystal.
So,

working at the appropriate time and phase of the
moon,
Cast a circle round following your own tradition or
cast a solo circle as outlined on pages 41- 42.

Firstly I bless and consecrate everything that I am
about to use by Earth, Air, Fire and Water. I do this by
passing it all through the smoke of an appropriate
incense and sprinkling it all lightly with salt water.
I conjure up within me a clear image of the person I
am healing and hold my intent clear.
Firstly I stitch the poppet round leaving only a small
opening, and while I stitch I charge the poppet. with
my intent, feeling my wishes flow into the stitches.
Then I fill the poppet with the mix of dried plants and
herbs that I have chosen, adding a small crystal if it
feels appropriate.
Next I stitch the poppet closed.
Features may be added to the poppet at this stage if it
aids your visualisation.
If the healing is for a woman I stitch on a piece of
willow, if it is for a man then add a piece of oak.
Once complete I name it, and then consecrate it by the
elements and charge it with one of the methods
suggested on the previous pages:

Poppet, Poppet ~
Carry true
All the energy
I charge to you

The poppet may then be linked to the person you are
healing using the linking circles visualisation, and
once the moon cycle is complete it can be put to rest
in the same way.

A Poppet for Protection

For protection I would use a white or silver fabric to reflect negativity away.
The stitching would generally be white.
Some of the protective herbs and plants that I would generally use to reflect away and provide protection would be:
Alder Bark
Angelica
Beech leaves
Betony
Birch twigs
Daffodil
Elder
Hyssop
Juniper
Mistletoe
Mugwort
Rosemary
Snap Dragon
Willow
I would also add a small piece of mirrored something.
The poppet would again be made within a circle cast at the appropriate phase of the moon.
Again everything to be used in the creation of the poppet should be blessed by the four elements.
At all times keep your intent clear in your mind.
Firstly sew the poppet round leaving only a small gap and with every stitch visualise your energy weaving a protective shimmering web around it. Next fill the poppet with a selection of dried plants and herbs and a reflective something and then stitch closed.
I would then personalize the poppet by giving it a face and if the protection is for a woman I stitch on a

piece of willow, if it is for a man then add a piece of
oak.
Name your poppet and then charge it and consecrate
it as before.

Poppet, Poppet ~
Carry true
All the energy
I charge to you

To link the poppet to the person, use the merging two
circles method but as you are creating a protection
not a healing, the intent and visualisation will need
amending:
To reflect negative energy away I would visualise a
circle of outward- facing mirrors surrounding each,
the poppet and the person, and then enlarge that into
a sparkling mirrored sphere.
The method would therefore be:

I place the poppet in my left hand, palm up,
and say/chant

"Be in a circle, it is protecting you"

I see the poppet within a mirrored sphere of light

In my right hand, palm up, I place a token to
represent the person I am working for
(a picture, or their name written on a piece of
parchment for example)
and say/chant

"Be in a circle, you are protected too"

I see the person within a mirrored sphere of light.

I then move my hands together until they are just
touching side by side and I can
See the two mirrored spheres overlapping
and say/chant

"Unite ~ Be as one"

I then fold my left hand onto my right, linking the
two hands together, linking the reflective and
protective energy of the poppet to the person and I
can See the two protective spheres merge into one
and say/chant

"Unite ~ Be as one"

To strengthen the protective and reflective powers of
the poppet further, a rhyme or your clear good
wishes may be inscribed on a small piece of bark or
parchment and placed inside the poppet prior to
stitching it closed.

Once the moon cycle is complete the poppet can be
put to rest in the same way, taken apart and the
pieces returned to the Earth.

Poppet, Poppet ~ Made by me,
Poppet, Poppet ~ you I see,
Poppet, Poppet ~ Charmed and blessed,
Poppet, Poppet ~ Now at rest,
At rest,
At rest.

As I mentioned before, the poppets I use most are those made out of what I gather as I walk within the landscape of the Cauldron. Although not being as traditional as the fabric or clay poppet, for me they work well and readily invoke the power of this land. Explore and find the style of poppet that works most readily for you.

Poppets have many uses. However, as always, remember to be open and clear with your intent, keep things as focused and as simple as possible. And remember only work for another with that person's full knowing permission.
This is for several reasons, but the most obvious are that people need to walk their own paths and learn their own lessons and *make their own choices*.
It is possible to inform and assist but not make decisions for them, no matter how well intentioned.

A Summer Walk....

The days are longest
The light is strongest
Elements shout loud to me as I walk this land

Air and fire
The sun- warmed breeze

Earth and water
The peat path I tread

I find shade beneath wide -spread branches of
an ancient oak
and kneel on soft fine grass,

I feel the sinking softness of the slightly damp
earth below me and welcome the connection,
I breathe out all tension and take the time to
become aware of all my senses...

To really feel, to really Be,
where I am

Right hand moves casting half circle from
knees in front to feet behind
Meets left hand behind me which completes the
casting of my solo circle by moving from feet
behind leftwards to knees in front

Fingers slowly releasing seeds and small pieces
of plant gathered on my route here repeat the
movement to overlay circle cast,
right hand from front to back
left hand from back to front,
small tokens of this task at hand

Thus thrice is circle cast as empty hands
inscribe once more

Empty hands then placed palms up on knees
I visualize the glow of a sphere surrounding me
I welcome each element as guardians of this
space

I open my senses

The air alive with the hum of insects
Dragonfly, shimmering brittle beauty of jewel
in flight with smaller damselfly as entourage
Butterflies in spiralling pairs over humid land
or feeding perched on sun- warmed flowers
Bees buzz from plant to plant harvesting
And spider webs shimmer, spun over tempting
fruit or flower

I welcome their spirits all

Circle is cast...

Touching the Elements

Working with the four elements is an important part of any magic. To feel them and know them, to be able to weave their attributes into your working is an important tool.

One way to get to know the elements is to meditate on each, to journey into the feel, the sense, of an element and what it can mean. This may most easily be experienced in a location that is appropriate to that element, preferably within your local environment, or if not then somewhere that holds a special meaning to you. For example,

Earth may be experienced seated on a ploughed field, or any bare earth, or leaning back against a rock face, or seated in a cave.

Air could be most felt in a very windy environment, be it at the summit of a hill or the top of a tower block. Work with Air at first when there is a definite breeze.

Fire can be meditated on any where in the bright sunshine on a sunny day, or by an open fire.

Water could be contemplated by sea or river or stream or pool, or being in the rain. Make the most of where you are, explore your environment and know it.

After each elemental meditation try to note down something about your experience. This could be a list of a few words, or a poem or a picture, or a journal entry of your process into the element, or a comment that sums up your emotions.

All responses to the elements can be very individual and it is this personalised knowing that allows you to weave the elements into your personal magic.

Allow time for the experience to embed itself into
your subconscious. Retouch each element as often as
you feel the need for more clarity over it, or simply if
a particular element calls to you, as you may need to
use that particular energy to bring more of a balance
within you.

You may want to bring a sense of completion to your
learning by undertaking a simple elemental
affirmation with each element after spending some
time getting to know it and touching it.
When undertaking an elemental affirmation be very
sensitive of the place that you choose. Different places
do have different feels to them, and special places
have a Spirit all of their own.

Work within a circle cast, and close your circle after.
A circle may by closed by placing palms to earth and
grounding the energy down, feel it flow from you,
and give your thanks.

Circle is closed…..

What follows is a brief introduction to touching the
four physical elements followed by some ideas
around elemental affirmation.

Earth

Roots & Nurturing
Rocks & Stability & Structure
Decay & Re brth
Crystals & Caverns
Home & Life

Find your place and cast your solo circle round...

I work with the element of Earth especially for magic
around the areas of nurturing, decay, rebirth, stability
and structure. However this list is not exclusive or in
any way exhaustive. To learn if Earth is appropriate
for what you wish to do ~ explore it!
This should be done on both material and non -
material levels. Physically touch the Earth, be it rock
or soil or crystal. Explore its texture, its shape and
structure and its warmth or chill, use all your senses
to actually **feel** the Earth, and let its energy ground
you. On the non- material level, find a place that
most represents the element of Earth to you, be it a
rock, a field, a cave or a quiet spot in your garden or
local park. I have done Earth meditations in fields, in
cellars and basements, in Long Barrows, sitting on the
ground in a garden and a park, in a cave and on a
large boulder at the edge of a building site. They have
all grounded me and connected me with Earth.
Cast your solo circle, either as simply outlined on
pages 41 – 42. Or as your own tradition teaches. As
always when working with the elements, call upon
Earth with clarity and care. Remember to close the
circle down after your meditation.

A Simple Earth Meditation

Make and keep contact with the Earth,
Touch bare skin to ground,
Be it foot or hand or the side of your face,
Close your eyes
Listen
To your heart beat
To the sounds around you

Breathe deep and slow
Let go of it all
Just feel, don't analyse

Breathe

Slow down
And relax

Imagine yourself sinking slowly into the Earth
Breathe deep
Send down roots, slowly grow down
Breathe deep and slow
Tap into the power of the Earth

Touch it
Feel it

Open to its warmth, to its nature

Experience it holding you
Supporting you
Giving

Breathe ~ Feel

Take as long as you need to relax into it.
To experience the support that it offers

Then
Follow the flow of energy up through your roots
Up into your centre

Acknowledge it
Welcome it

This is Earth.

Air

Breeze & Wind
Speech & Song
Communication & Community
Flight & Movement
Breathe & Life

Find your place and cast your solo circle round…

I work with the element of Air when I am working
with issues of communication or miscommunication,
misunderstandings, gossip or general confusion.
I work with Air to provide clarity, and also when
dealing with movement or travel.
For me communication is extremely important, it is at
the heart of all relationships and all communities
Words are powerful, however we do not
communicate solely with words.
For communication to work one needs to listen to
more than the bare words that are being spoken.
One also needs to listen beyond one's own
preconceptions. In this way you can be open to new
experiences, new possibilities:

Air, movement, breathe, life, song, meaning.

To know and experience Air on a physical level find a
place where you can feel the wind in your face or
where you can hear its power as it sweeps through
trees or reeds or grasses. This could be on an open
plain, at the top of a hill or the top of a tower block or
standing by tall trees, wherever Air is most obvious to
you.

I have done an Air meditation equally effectively on the balcony of a tower block in London, on the top of the Tor in Glastonbury, at the viewing point at the top of Ebbor Gorge, on the edge of a cliff facing the sea, and at the top of a swaying tree in a city park.

Find a space where the Air sings to you, physically out stretch your arms, face into it and let it blow around you, breathe in, let it refresh you.
Feel its motion, its chill or warmth, its caress against your skin, hear the sound of its passing.

Cast your solo circle, either as simply outlined on pages 41 – 42 or as your own tradition teaches, as always when working with the elements call upon Air with clarity and care and remember to close the circle down after your meditation.

A Simple Air Meditation

Face into the breeze, or into the wind
Let it caress the skin of your face
Let it blow through your unbound hair
Or caress the curves of your skull if hair has
departed

Hear it sweeping past your ears
Close your eyes
Listen
Experience the sound of Air passing
Hear and feel its passage
Feel and hear the movement

Raise and outstretch your arms
Bare your arms to its flow

Breathe deep and slow
Let go of everything filling your mind
Let the wind blow it away
Feel
Don't analyse

Breathe
Slow down
And relax

Imagine yourself leaning into the strength of the
wind
Letting it fill you
Letting it support you
Letting it carry you

Breathe

Open to the nature of Air
Experience the changes within the flow and
movement of it

Let it carry you

Let it give to you

Breathe

Take as long as you need to relax into it
To experience all that the element of Air may
offer to you
To experience its fluidity and potential

Breathe

Lower your arms
Bow your head
And feel the energy
Deep in your centre

Acknowledge it
Welcome it

This is Air.

Fire

Sun & Lightning Strike
Purification & Rebirth
Clearing & Light
Transformation & Change
Heat & Life

Find your place and cast your solo circle round...

I work with Fire most when I am focusing on clearing and transformation ~ and during rites of purification. If you want help dealing with sudden changes in your life then the energy of Fire may also be of assistance.

To experience Fire you need only stand out in the heat of the midday sun in summer, or watch a sunrise, or sit before that roaring fire in winter. If you live close to an old- fashioned forge with a friendly Smith or near to volcanic activity for true Fire of Earth that would be doubly magical.

If all the above are impossible for you then in a clear space in your home sit within a circle of safely placed candles in secure holders ~ as ever with fire, respect is the key word.

In the Fire meditation obviously do not look directly at the sun or actually touch the fire.

Use your eyes to explore Fire. Look at the heat haze raised by the heat of the sun, look at the flames of the fire, look at the glowing coals or embers their colour, their movement.

Experience the smell of its presence and its passing. How do you respond to heat, or the lack of it? Have you listened to the sound of fire?

Cast your solo circle, either as simply outlined on
pages 41 – 42. or as your own tradition teaches. As
always when working with the elements call upon
Fire with clarity and care. Remember to close the
circle down after your meditation.

A Simple Fire Meditation

Face your fire

(And if it is not the Sun…)

Look at the energy of light it gives
Look at the movement of the flames
Their shifting colour and shape

Breathe deep and slow
Slow down
Relax

Reach out your bare hands toward it
Experience the energy it generates as heat
Feel the warmth caress you
(Do not actually touch the fire ~ the energy it
radiates is enough!)

Breathe deep and slow
Breathe in the warm air

Smell it, taste it
Just feel, don't analyse

Breathe

Slow down
And relax

Listen

Acknowledge the sounds that surround you.
Then let them go one by one until you only hear
Fire
Its movement, its passing

Breathe deep and slow

Accept the power of Fire
Fully experience it
Welcome it in

Feel the Fire within you
Feel it grow and strengthen
Feel yourself glowing with Fire

Breathe
Relax
Be

Feel the spark inside your mind
Welcome the flame

The energy
The power

Welcome Fire

Take as long as you need to experience Fire.
To know, to learn all that the element of Fire may
offer to you at this time,
Let it swirl and spiral into your centre
Let it focus
Welcome it, acknowledge it

This is Fire.

Then
Let the energy go,
Lower your hands turn your palms downwards
Let the energy of fire
Flow from you

Feel its cleansing passage as it departs
Be refreshed and renewed

Know Fire.

Water

Rain & Sea & Ice & Flood
Nurturing & Growth
Transition & Support
Tides & Movement
Emotion & Life

Find your place and cast your solo circle round…

I work with the element of Water when I am working with emotions, whether to soothe anger or nurture love or to create calm. Emotions can be deep or shallow, fluid or still.

The element of Water may also be used when weaving magic for growth and nurturing.

Water can also symbolise transition or movement, both from one place to another and one emotion to another. Water carries you, emotionally and physically, and Water moves to the rhythm of the tides.

Water may be explored on a beach where the impact of the tides is very obvious or by a river or canal where the flows are more varied and seasonal.

Ponds or pools or lakes in the landscape are also ideal places, be they natural or man made, large or small. They are places of containment and slower movement. Water may also be experienced at a waterfall, in a shower, in a bath or on a boat.

Do not feel limited or restricted by where you are, make the most of it.

If the only way available to you to focus on the element of Water is to sit there with a small bowl of it in your hands then do that..

It will obviously not be as easy as if you were standing in the waves at the edge of the sea, however you will still be able to experience the element.

Physically touch the water, let it flow through your fingers, feel how it moves.
Study it with your eyes, follow any ripples, see the patterns and see the distortions it can create as it bends the light. Is it fresh or stale, does it have a scent or a colour? Use all your senses and if you know it is safe to do so, then taste it. If it is not safe to drink or you are unsure then when you next get the chance to drink fresh water really focus on how it tastes, but also how it feels as it flows into you.

Cast your solo circle, either as simply outlined on pages 41 – 42 or as your own tradition teaches, as always when working with the elements call upon Water with clarity and care. It is important to remember to close the circle down after your meditation.

A Simple Water Meditation

*Face your water
Let it caress your skin
Let it touch you in movement and in stillness*

*Close your eyes
Feel
Experience the caress of it
Feel and hear and fully smell and sense the
movement*

*Breathe slow and deep
Let go of everything filling your mind
Let the water carry it away
Feel the release
Don't analyse
Let go*

*Breathe
Slow down
And relax*

*Imagine yourself being within the strength of the
water ~ floating*

Let it caress you
Let it support you
Let it carry you

Breathe

Open to the nature of Water
Experience the changes within the flow and
movement of it

Let it carry you
Let it give to you
Let it nurture you

Breathe

Take as long as you need to relax into it
To experience all that the element of Water may
offer to you
To experience its fluidity and potential

Breathe
Feel Water's energy flowing deep into your
centre

Acknowledge it
Welcome it

This is Water.

Elemental Affirmation

When you have been working with the elements for a while you may find a need within you to acknowledge that learning. If this is the case then the symbolism of an elemental affirmation may be appropriate.

With any affirmation, deep fears and/ or emotions may surface and it is wise to be safe and ensure that there is someone to watch over you, wait for you and support you afterwards. It should be remembered that it is not always safe to spend time out [especially at night] on your own.

For an affirmation I would suggest that you take a trip to somewhere special that is very representative of the element that you are going to be working with. For example:
An Earth affirmation at a cave
An Air affirmation at a geographical high point
A Fire affirmation at a working forge
A Water affirmation on a beach

It should be a place at which an element
strongly calls to
YOU

When you decide to go, remember to take with you a gift or token that will naturally fade back into the landscape and anything that you need to cast your circle, as well as sensible clothing that is appropriate for wherever you are going to be.

The purpose of the affirmation is to recognise and acknowledge your connection to a particular element.

As an affirmation you are going to spend time with that element. The length of time is up to you, however as an example the last Earth affirmation that I was present at lasted over night. Others have lasted just an hour or two. Warn those who are going to be with you!

So firstly find a space that to you creates a sacred link to the element you will be working with. Cast your circle round using the method that you are most comfortable with.

Then
carry out a simple meditation on the element to take you on from the physical place of the element into the mind space or spiritual space where you connect strongly to it.
Stay there.

Breath deep and focus.

Call on the element directly to affirm the connection

For example:

By all of Earth that touches me
By soil, by stone, by bone
By all of Earth that is deep in me
By soil, by stone, by bone,
I ask you now to speak with me
By soil, by stone, by bone.

Or

By all of Water that touches me
by blood, by thirst, by tears
By all of Water that is deep in me
by blood, by thirst, by tears
I ask you now to speak with me
by blood, by thirst, by tears

Then
LISTEN

You may find that you are challenged.
Fears may rise up deep inside you
fear of the space where you are
fear of the element that you are working with
Look at your fear, recognise it, accept it, own it.

[This is one reason for having someone there to watch over
*you, so that in the material reality you **are** safe.]*

You may find that you are given the gift of an image
or a vision
Give thanks for it.

You may find that you receive a physical gift
representative of the element or the space that you are
working with.
Give thanks for it.

Listen until the energy of the element
permeates all of you.
Acknowledge that it is always present both within
you and surrounding you.
Then slowly

take time to release the energy of the element back
from you into the environment surrounding you,
while affirming your continued link to it.

Give your gift.

Close your circle.

And take some time to record your experience.

Don't try to analyse it yet, just create as full and
accurate a record as possible. Let the words or
pictures flow from you, the element may still be
speaking. Then let whom ever is with you take care of
you and get you to eat and drink.

Affirmations can be powerful experiences and should
not be undertaken lightly. They should only happen
after you are already very familiar with all of the
elements. This ensures balance.

Every affirmation will be different, simply because all
the elements have different properties, and the
manner in which you as an individual relate to them
will be extremely personal. The affirmation is likely to
confront you with your own fears and with your
points of strength, both of which you may previously
have been unaware of or have been ignoring.
Honour such messages, as they are areas for you to
develop and work with within your magic.

Occasionally, a landscape or sacred space will touch you deeply and unexpectedly and an affirmation may occur in an almost spontaneous manner.

The Somerset Levels, the Cauldron of Avalon, did this to me. Utterly unplanned on one of my very first visits to the Cauldron I experienced the very deep call of the element of Water. I walked out toward the wide pool of water that was calling to me and in the midst of the rain I carried out an affirmation. It was a very wet and windswept hedgewitch who returned to her friends some while later with a head full of images and words. It was only much later after I had moved here that I researched the area I had worked at that day and discovered that the flooded landscape creating the pool that had called and spoken so strongly to me was the site of the Meare Pool.
[see page 104]
Therefore trust your instincts, and feel the elements that are woven throughout the landscape, no matter where you are.

Take time.

An Early Autumn Walk....

As I walk, eyes scanning almost without
thought the horizon, I see the colours
that surround me and theirs is the first
deep impact:
Deep grey sky looming over golden reeds
embedded in the mirror of black water
framed by the short green vegetation
before me.
No blending of the greens of majestic
broadleaf woodland here, rather colours
that harmonise through their dramatic
contrasts, dominated by gold and black,
my black- lined amber chalice,
replete with still water
perfect for scrying...

Scrying

Scrying is a tool and a skill. Like many things it may be instantly accomplished by some with a talent in that direction, or it can take patience and practise to acquire.

It took me practise to regain the skill I had as that child often chided for being distracted. It can take time to move beyond the surprise at the first appearance of an image, which jolts you back into the here and now with the thought of

"I can see something!"

You need to just let the image sink into your awareness.

Scrying can be used to ask for guidance with making a decision, to obtain an answer to a puzzle or a question, it can be used to look into potential futures or the darkness of the past. In some ways scrying can be similar to and used as, a form of meditation.

Scrying means different things to different people and because of that is used and performed in many different ways. Although I tend to use a pool, the classical examples are obviously the crystal ball and, slightly less common, the black mirror. A plain silvered mirror or a polished piece of metal may also be used for scrying however these are usually combined with candles for illumination.

I try to use scrying at the in between times, at dusk and at dawn, these are magical times and I find my scrying more successful then, however any time will do when there is a need.

When you visit a place repeatedly to scry, the very walk to that place will begin to help you with the transition into the state of mind needed to be successful. This is one reason that I always try to keep to the same route when I am going to visit the pool that I am currently using for scrying. The same thing occurs when you use a particular bowl over and over again, the entire process of the cleansing and filling up with water of that specific bowl will aid you. What is happening is the creation of a practical ritual to quiet your mind and transfer your focus from the physical realms to the realms beyond.

Find a pool of still water: this can be the edge of a lake, a rock pool when the tide is out, a pool or dew pond, a deep puddle in the woods or high up on the moors, it can be the pond in your back garden or the local park, a bowl of water you place on the table, or even, in an emergency, that puddle on the pavement…

To Scry...

*Kneel before your pool, listen to the sounds that
surround you, accept them, be calm with them
and just let them be and fade into the background
as you focus on the sounds within, your breath,
physical qualities, the physical manifestation of
you, all that your body feels, acknowledge it,
slow down.*

*Close your eyes and 'feel' what is surrounding
you. Not just hear / touch / smell but reach out
with your mind to 'feel' your surroundings, no
judgements just awareness,
slow down.*

*Open your eyes and gaze into the black water,
open your eyes and let your sight open,
slow down.*

*It may be images
in the ripples that cross the surface
It may be something in the depth of the pool,
be open, be receptive,
carry no preconceptions of what might occur*

It may be the token of a leaf or feather that drifts toward you,
It may be the sudden image in your mind's eye
Close your eyes and breathe deep and sense all that surrounds you.

Open your eyes and gaze at the dark waters

What gifts from the Divine?

Repeat this process as often as you feel inclined, for me this is usually a minimum of three times until the focus comes and only inner perception remains.
When you feel completion, bring the palms of your hands to your eyes, to seal them, and then put palms to earth to ground. Breathe in deeply and then release your breath with a low gentle sound to break the link with the outer silence. Break the surface of your scrying pool with pebble, twig or hand. Sit back, and if you want to or need to, write any notes. Feel the sense of calm or sometimes jump up and down because you've just realised how cold it actually is and how long you have been there!
Now is when you want that practical person with the flask of hot drink in their bag...

Interpretation

Sometimes what you see will have an obvious association for you. You may see yourself in a certain place or at a certain event or moving toward or away from something. At other times things may not be that clear, you may see something that at first glance appears to not be relevant to you or connected with the question. Do not discard these as irrelevant, as the mind works strongly with symbolism ~ these images may just need some thought or interpretation:

What does that symbol represent?
Does that plant have a meaning?
Does that animal/bird/insect represent a Goddess or God or hold another meaning?

Once you begin to accept all the images with an open mind, your scrying should flow more, just acknowledge them and note them for future interpretation. Sometimes the image that you see could hold a meaning totally personal to you, due to associations built in your childhood for example, so trust those interpretations just as much as correspondences from books!
Possible meanings for plants and trees were mentioned earlier on pages 16 – 25 , meanings for some common animals and birds are on pages 71- 74. Use these representations to begin the process of interpreting your visions, but remember they are only a guide. Creatures that you notice as you walk to your scrying place may also have a relevance to your vision; their crossing your path may be serendipitous.

Wild life

Some simple meanings associated with the more common local animals and insects

Badger ~

A badger will confront all foes and as such represents the archetypal hero. A warrior and a setter of boundaries.

Butterfly ~

In Cornwall the folk lore is that white butterflies are the souls of the dead. Magical messengers and teachers of transformation, they are sacred to Aphrodite and Psyche.

Bee ~

Bees know all. They can help in becoming the centre of attention in a positive manner. Sacred to Melissa, Aphrodite and Demeter, they are creatures of harvest and preservation. In Egypt they were known as the tears of Ra.

Deer & Stag ~

These animals are sacred to Herne. They are Otherworld messengers, fey, and of the twilight, of dusk and of dawn. They are of great power, and strength .and both challenge and protect.

Dove ~

A symbol of peace, healing and love.

Dragonfly ~

Traditionally connected to the fairy folk, these fairy steeds may travel between the realms. They are symbols of protective mirage and illusion. Dragonflies also represent transformation and the gaining of wisdom through change. Metamorphosis creating maturation, letting go of, but learning from, the past. Dragonfly may also be used as a representation of Dragon energy.

Fox ~

A fox is adaptable and can also symbolise awareness and cunning.

Frog ~

Sacred to Isis, Aphrodite, Venus and Hecate frogs represent new life rebirth and resurrection, also initiation.

Hare ~

A symbol of fertility and often thought to be a witch's familiar because of the suddenness of its movements, making it seem to vanish and reappear.
Hares can also become 'moonstruck' and are therefore used as symbols for moon magic and scrying.

Hedgehog ~

In folk lore the Hedgehog is a fairy steed. It symbolizes defence and keeping all at bay, a shield.

Heron ~

Standing for long stretches of time along the banks of rivers and rhynes, the Heron symbolises silence, vigilance,

quietness and thought or contemplation. The Fisher King
and symbol of the renewal of life, the Heron is the bird of
Osiris.

Kestral ~

Hovering in freedom from the movement of the Air while
incorporating all its energy, this little falcon symbolises
travel and movement across all planes. It is a creature of
the Sun and of freedom and traditionally connected with
Odin.

Mouse ~

A symbol of abundance who can teach us how to keep a low
profile.

Owl ~

Representative of death, night and the balance of opposites,
Owls are sacred to Athena and Diana. They are symbols of
wisdom and learning the entire truth. Diplomats and
messengers old and wise.

Rabbit ~

These animals represent abundance and community,
organisation and unity.

Raven, Crow & Magpie ~

All of these are birds of the Morrigan and as such represent
the Otherworld, mysticism, magic and protection.

Spider ~

Weaver of fates, and a reminder of the connectedness of all things and how one action may have unforeseen consequences. The web can also be taken as a reminder to not become entangled in the illusion of the material world.

Squirrel ~

Representative of materialism, a Squirrel also confronts problems head on.

Swan ~

These beautiful creatures represent fidelity and faithfulness. They are of Brigid, Aphrodite and Venus. Weave their feathers into charms for strength and protection and to find clarity.

Toad ~

These are sacred to Hekate, with strong underworld connections, and symbolise the growth of your psychic nature.

Pools & Moon Magic

Scrying by the light of the moon, especially the full moon, can be a very powerful experience.
To view the slow transit of the reflection of the moon across water is to travel through a different type of time, ~ it is crossing the veils. Visions experienced at such times can be particularly clear and potent.
However magic incorporating the reflection of the moon in water is not limited to scrying.
There is a long tradition of healing and magic using such reflections and indeed drawing on the energy of the moon in such manner is a powerful evocation of the Divine feminine.
Within a magic circle, (cast as you would generally cast a circle according to whatever tradition you follow or if you would like cast a simple solo circle as shown on pages 41-42) a bowl filled with water is placed to catch the moonlight, so that the image of the face of the full moon may be viewed in the bowl.
This image of the moon is then used as the focal point to draw on and focus the moons energy. The moon water may have salt sprinkled into it to banish illness or appropriate magical herbs or plants may be added to aid a healing or strengthen the magic that you are working. A chant or rhyme may then be said to help as you study the reflection of the Moon in the water, and a wand (or a pointed finger) then used to stir and swirl the image.

She of the tides
She with full face glowing
She from whom no magic hides
She the ever knowing...

I call on you

She of the tides
She with full face glowing
She from whom no magic hides
She the ever knowing...

I call on you
To charge and bless

She of the tides
She with full face glowing
She from whom no magic hides
She the ever knowing...

I call on you
To charge and bless
This water who you rule

The Moon-charged water can then be used in several ways, such as:

★ Placing your hands within the water and then with your intent clear within you, using it to sprinkle or flick over the person [or the thing or the animal,] that you are healing or magically working for

★ Placing an image or token of what or whom you are healing or working for into the water and leaving it there for an appropriate amount of time

★ Visualise the water flowing over the person (or whatever you are working to heal) carrying with it all the energy of the Moon and all you have charged it with

In the end always return the water to the earth with thanks to all for their blessings. The bowl that you use to hold the water may be made of anything, however a small round mirror placed in its base will enhance the image of the moon. Or try a bowl with a smooth black inner surface that will reflect as a dark mirror reflects. A silver bowl can also be very appropriate as silver is the metal of the moon.

If you work outside around a pool of still water, or at the edge of such a pool, then the bowl used to reflect and contain the image of the moon may itself be floated on water creating a very intense link and strong charge.
Do be prepared to get wet though ~ retrieving the bowl being not always the simplest of tasks.

The blessings of the Moon may be drawn into items by floating them on water under a full moon in this manner. Charging items with the power of the moon in this way evokes the gentle flowing yet insistent strength of the changing tides and phases of the moon. Poppets and charms may both be enhanced by this floating, as will anything that would generally be left out in moonlight for a while.
Moon magic can be very intense, and yet also full of illusion, seeing by moonlight is seeing by reflection.

Chants, Rhymes and Rhythms...

Chants and rhymes help you to focus on the task at hand, they help you to clarify your intent, aiding you in being clear and to the point about your wishes and exactly what it is you are trying to achieve. They provide a focal point for your intent and a focus for the energy you are raising and channelling.

I tend to sit and think about what it is I am trying to achieve while I am thinking of the person I intend to work for, and if my intent is clear enough then a rhyme soon follows. I try to incorporate the name of the person I am working for along with the end result that I am aiming for or the transition that I want to induce.

Magical numbers are also a way to clarify your ideas, and are a good way to build a chant or spell, think about the traditional chant:

> "By the power of one............
> By the power of two....
> By the power of three..." etc.

and adapt. It to your need, for example:

> "By the power of one is the magic begun
> By the power of two good luck will find you
> By the power of three so it will be
>
> Etc.

Also look to the elements for inspiration, one of the simplest and most powerful chants I have ever used is the well known

'By the elements fourfold, in the fifth my spell shall hold.'

Calling upon the aid of an appropriate Goddess or God is another idea, if that is where your path leads you. If all else fails just forget about rhythms and state your intent. For example:

'May this help Anne heal'

As long as your intent is good and clear, and your wishes strong, then all will be well.

There are many rhythms that flow through this world and through our lives, those of the day, and those of the moon, those of the stars and planets and those of the seasons.
Different rhythms or flows may feel appropriate for individual charms or wishes or spells. For example:
It may be appropriate to work with the Moon phases if you are aware that the person you wish to assist has strong connections with the Moon.
These phases and flows of the moon can be incorporated or mixed into your magic very easily.
On the simplest level a growing waxing moon for adding and creation, a waning shrinking moon for removal and banishment.

Full and dark moons have their own associations and can be seen both as times of high energy and as times of null energy or transition. I see both as dynamic times of transition.

☽○☾

On a deeper astronomical level it is possible to link the Moon with the sign that it is passing through at the time and incorporate that flow and movement of energy into your spell craft.

Different times of the day have different associations according to different magical traditions. Most commonly, midday corresponds to a full moon and midnight to the dark of the moon but follow the correspondences that your path suggests, remembering that the quietest and calmest times are often at night.

Astrological correspondences are also powerful tools to work with, as are the energies of the different seasons and festivals. The flow of the stars and of the planets and seasons from spring through summer, autumn, winter and returning once more to spring area never ending cycles that take time to know but create deep under laying rhythms that can be woven into your magic once you can recognise them.

Basically begin to explore the rhythms and flows of the world around you, do not expect to be able to take them all into account at once. Experience will help you discover those you are most in tune with, and from that beginning you may explore the others.

Where and how you live may affect which rhythms
appear strongest to you.
When I lived in the city, the Moon was a clear and
distinct rhythm and had the strongest pull for me.
Now in the countryside where the seasons are clearer
and I can more easily walk the land, it is easier for me
to draw on that rhythm and flow for both energy and
inspiration, weaving it with the power of the sun and
moon, day and night and so on.

Keep notes on when you feel most creative,
on when you have most energy and on when you feel
most magical or most secure in your magic. Such a
journal may help you to better understand the
magical rhythms that flow both around you and
through you. As your understanding of these
rhythms grows you will be able to work with them,
and not accidentally in contradiction to them.

Work with the tradition that you are used to, and
keep to the familiar until you become confident and
more practised with what you are trying to create.
The more comfortable you are with what you are
trying to do the easier it will become to focus with
greater clarity and depth on your intent, and your
ability to feel the flow of rhythms both within you
and around you will increase.

A Winter Walk....

My breath is visible on the air
as I walk on ground that crunches and
crackles as I pass.
Chill wind greets me and the landscape
is bright and sparkling shades of silver
grey, reflections everywhere.
Bare branches reach toward the sky and
cast stark shadows in the winter sun,
and I am wary of the slipperiness of ice
on rock as I cross the slab of stone over
rhyne, whose edges are blurred with a
mosaic of crystals.
I cross the boundary into the woodland.
Less dark now than in Summer's
greenness, I follow the narrow path that
leads me soon to my destination; the old
tree that still stands though split
asunder with age...
my Gateway.

I walk the woodlands at all seasons, however in Winter the pathways ~ though muddy ~ are often more clearly visible. You can see the reality of the place without its bright disguise of greenery. I find this allows me to learn the lay of the land and explore places that become hidden once the wood is in full bloom. Obviously this is less true for stands of evergreen trees whose eternal cover keeps down the plants below it. Woodland within the Cauldron has a feel different to any I have walked elsewhere. It has taken on the feel of the soft, almost floating peat below it, and although the trees are slowly transforming the land, rooting and solidifying it, that sense of movement, of floating remains.

Walk the woods and sense them, try to get a feel of the overall nature of the woodland, its individuality as an entity in its own right. Is it a quiet, calm place, or one that is full of rustling noise that stresses its restlessness? Does it feel welcoming or is there an edge of danger or of mischief? Does this feeling change over the time of the day and the seasons? Give the woodland your time and your silence and visit it as the year warms from winter to spring to summer to autumn. It is only after a full cycle of seasons that it is possible to begin to fully appreciate the beauty and bounty and magic of a landscape, especially a wood. If where you live is devoid of woodland then be aware of those individual trees living around you, and acknowledge them.

As it takes time to get to know a person, so it takes time to know a place. Though occasionally one may instantly see the potential.

Betweens

Crossroads, gateways and windows,
are all between places neither here nor there
just as dusk and dawn are between times
neither light nor dark.

As such they hold magic.
These are good times and places to work magic.

Walk into the twilight of the Cauldron
and emerge renewed...

Crossroads

Decision points, options and choices.

Crossroads, these will appear many times in your life, both on material and on Spiritual /emotional levels. Crossroads, especially in my case three-branched crossroads, have always been magical spots. It is another case of working with the energy that is contained within the landscape.

They are somewhere you *have* to make a decision, which way will you proceed? These are places of choice.

Crossroads take many forms, anywhere three or four or more paths join. They may be main roads or back roads, tracks or droves, footpaths or pathways. They are a meeting of the ways or a parting of the ways. The older the place, the stronger it is likely to hold this energy because it will have been used as a point of choice or a destination by so many more travellers. Choose your crossroads with as much care as you can. Take time to *feel* the crossroads that surround you until you find the one that feels appropriate to the decision that you need to make, be it one of green pathways, rolled stone ways or tarmac roads. Crossroads are one of the between places, they are a place in themselves but also a place of movement, of transition. The time to work at crossroads is times that have a similar feel, such as dusk and dawn, sunrise and sunset, the between times.

These places can be used to bring into focus questions that come into your life. For example, I may work at crossroads when overwhelmed by a decision , asking for guidance from the place, the land.

At a three -branched crossroads I would ask for guidance from the Lady of the crossroads and leave offerings for her there. In many paths and traditions, the Lady of the crossroads is invoked to guide at times of passing and major rites of passage throughout life.

The lady of the crossroads:

Seen as a triple goddess form she incorporates
Maiden, Mother and Crone.
She is all phases of the moon, the full, the dark and
the times of change between.
She is of the earth, the sky and the underworld
She is at the beginning and the end of all things and
guides our footsteps in between.

If we ask
and if we are prepared
to listen.

I cast my circle at the crossroads and
invoke the energy of the elements and of the Divine.
I call on the energy of the place as my guide and I
allocate each path of the crossroads with an answer to
my question or an option or decision.
Then I see which way calls.

Some of the ways of working with the energy of
crossroads in this way are:

★ Placing a candle on each path that is charged by
anointing it with oil while thinking of the option or
choice that it will represent and observing which
burns in an unusual manner,
or simply which one remains alight.

★ Use a pendulum and see which path calls most
positively to you.

★ Focus on the energy of the place, close your eyes,
allow your breath to take up the rhythm of the space,
the meeting of the paths, link yourself to it,
visualise yourself sending down roots into the
crossroads
Root yourself within the place, then
ask your question clearly within your mind
and open your eyes and look.
Does one particular path glow or glisten?
Does a guide await you?
Take time and the answer will come.

Always remember to give thanks for the guidance
given and once asked for always consider any
response received seriously.

As the crossroad is a between place so it may hold
things between times and between places for you. It
can become a place of awaiting and a place of secrets.
In these circumstances I would again work within a
circle, invoking the energy of the elements and the
Divine. I would then give that which I wish to remain
hidden to the crossroads to hold, either by inscribing
it onto bark or parchment and burying it there,
or by physically placing something you wish hidden
at the crossroads.

At important times of change and development
within your life it may be appropriate to consider
leaving a gift of acknowledgement and thanks at a
crossroads, for example after a birth, a handfasting or
a death. Remember to not leave a gift that is not at
one with the earth and will not return naturally and
safely to it. It may be appropriate to create a specific
token as you walk to the crossroads. Think on what
you are doing and leave nothing that will mar the
spot or trap or entangle wildlife.

I seek your power, Lady of the shadows
I call on your strength,
Lady of three roads,
I ask your wisdom, Lady who knows.

And that this all may now begin
I welcome you in
I welcome you in
I welcome you in.

Gateways

Transitions: from one place to the next, to where?

Gateways are another decision point, a point of transition and neither here nor there, a half -hidden point where you may stand *between* two places, not quite in one or the other. That is their power, the shadow spaces, the in betweens, like dusk and dawn, the twilights.

They are a good place to study and think on the boundaries that surround you in life, a good place for letting go of the old and stepping into the new. Work with gateways when you want to expand your boundaries or when you want to create a complete change. The act of stepping through a physical gateway from the present into your future on a magical level may well create and support the mind set that you require to achieve and maintain such a change within your life.

You are creating the potential.

Gateways may also allow you to *see* your potential. When you stand at the threshold, waiting within the gateway, you can see what has led you to this point and also glimpse what lays before.

Any gate, doorway or arch will do, anything that is a specific gap or entrance or exit. But some may be more appropriate to the work you wish to do, and some may be easier to use than others. If it is an old gateway then that may help as it will hold the energy of having been used many times for coming and going. However the new may also contain power so do not immediately discount them, especially if one particular location draws you.

If it is firmly within the structure of a building then it may be most suitable for looking at or performing transitions on the material level, for example changing jobs, stepping away from a bad habit or stepping toward a more positive life choice.

If it is in a ruin or standing alone, then because it is separate, because it is free of physical boundaries, it may be used for more emotional and magical transitions, for example moving forward onto a new path, leaving behind a time of regrets or stepping into a more creative or positive mindset.

Gateways may also provide entrance into the realms of the Fey, the otherworld. These gateways may be harder to find ~ they are the gap through a split tree, or under a fallen bough shrouded with the curtain of ivy. They are both transitory and ancient.

Look at what is around you. What doorways, what gateways are present?

It should also be remembered that gateways may well have gatekeepers. These may be both guardians and protectors of a gateway or guides.

A password or clear intention or question may be needed to gain passage through the gateway.

ଔ◯ଞ

At Dusk or Dawn
At twilight
At the between times
When all is filled with change
Kneel before your chosen gateway
and cast your circle round.

Stand now and calm your heartbeat
Breath in this place, this time
Open all your senses

Know this place, *feel* its power.

With open eyes explore your gateway
Its shape
Its size
Its realm

Match it to your desire
And ask your wish out loud
State with clear intent
Speak truth
No room for shades of doubt

Give time
to *hear* an answer
or challenge to your request

Give time and give your answer
Speak from your heart
Not from your head

Open now your gateway
With chant and moving hands
Step forward onto threshold
Into the Otherland.

Look forward at the new horizons
Visualise, see your goal achieved
Experience new boundaries
And now
Believe.

Open all your senses

Know this place *feel* its power

Believe
Step forward
Claim your place and claim your power
Feel the change within you
Hold it
Know it
Be it.

~ Now ~

Still looking forward
Still feeling sure and strong
Open up your circle
And step beyond…

Standing at the threshold
I raise my hands before me palms outstretched
to push open the door.
I remove all obstructions
from my chosen path....

May all that I want go with me
All else I freely leave behind

Window Magic

*You can see any where and any when through the right
window, and perhaps create a future...*

Window magic is all about seeing what may be,
And maybe manifesting what you want to be...

As it is all about potential, it is also a between times
magic. However unlike crossroads and gateways,
window magic is more in tune with dawn and sunrise
and the waxing phase of the moon.

Use window magic for looking into possible futures,
for looking at possible outcomes. It is a *"what if..."*
type of magic that allows you to explore the
possibilities of your actions or choices. The nature of
windows is to be looked through and so the magic of
them is also looking, it is very akin to scrying.

Windows may reveal much and help with
visualisations for manifestation as you can welcome
into your life a particular view from your particular
window.
Windows may be used from the inside looking out or
the outside looking in. They may be in houses, offices,
ruined warehouses, or castles. Windows may be in
rusting cars or doll houses or barns. Most man- made
structures, modern or old, contain windows and
therefore hold the potential for window magic.

If you are searching for someone, choose a window
that overlooks people or used to. If you are searching
for a possible outcome involving travel or movement,

then choose a window that overlooks or overlooked a
well-travelled path or road.

Basically find a window that gives you a view that
relates to your question. It is the view that is
important although what the window is in may also
be relevant. For example I would choose one within
an older building to look at the past and one within a
newer for the present, but if you find a window in a
quiet place that draws you to it, no matter where it is,
if it has the right view it will serve.

To See

Choose your window with care and choose an
appropriate time
Get close to your window
If there is a windowsill big enough, sit on it
You want to be *close* to the window
and focus on the feel of it.

Cast your circle round
Feel the energy of the elements surround you
and fill you.
In your mind or in reality
drape a curtain over your window

Stop
Breathe
Slow down
Close your eyes
Ask your question, ask "What if…"
Focus only on that
Focus all of you on the question
Open your eyes
Draw back the curtain
and look through…

It may be a sign,
It may be a symbol,
It may be a vision

However, it is a lot like scrying in that it takes time to
develop this skill. If nothing appears close your eyes
and ask again
Give of your time
Give of your patience
Acknowledge any images
but do not analyse
Feel
And accept.

Close the circle

And then make notes.

Windows may be opened
and windows may be closed.
Through an open window you may pick
something from your future and bring it to the
present as a symbol.

Through a *natural* window
You may look into the otherworld...

A willow view of water on the levels,
an oak view of a road on the hill
a yew tree window at Samhain...

Magic in the landscape.

The Cauldron Of Avalon

I stand on this land of evermore
This Summerland of
the Avalon Marshes
and I am in a Cauldron of rebirth. The cauldron
is a symbol of plenty, of fertility
Of life everlasting
and rebirth after death.

The Avalon Marshes
are a fertile green land
Transformed
and reclaimed from the sea.
They are peat, the decayed remains of former
plants
literally,
Life reborn from death.

☽○☾

The Cauldron of Avalon
Conclusion in the landscape

Within every landscape there is a story of transition and change with the new overlaying the old, rivers migrate, as do people and industry. This has an impact on the feel, the energy that a place has. Areas that have stayed the same over long periods of time have a more solid feel to them than those continually in change where the knowledge of the landscape and its potential may be lost or hidden.

Explore the hidden landscapes of where you live, uncover the roots of the present and ground your magic there. Integrate, feel the lay of the land, its geography, and weave yourself into it. By exploring the history of where you are, by finding out how the land around you has changed you will be able to ground both yourself and your magic deep within it, present and past.

The Cauldron of Avalon that I know has a physical reality within the local landscape. With its open mouth to the Severn Estuary its sides are delineated by the Polden and Mendip hills, and the higher ground surrounding Street, Glastonbury and Wells form its base (see Map One).
The cauldron as a symbol of femininity, fertility, transformation and rebirth reaches back into the myths of many cultures, from Egyptian to Indian to Scandinavian to Celtic … to mention but a few.
The Egyptian Book of the Dead shows the hieroglyph of the Deep that gives birth to the Universe and the Gods as a representation of three cauldrons. The three cauldrons of cosmic creation are also present within

Map One

*Map of the Cauldron showing approximate
location of 10 metre above sea level contour line*

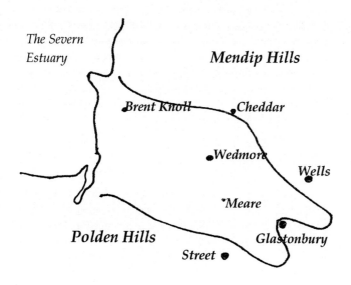

*The Severn
Estuary*

Mendip Hills

.Brent Knoll — .Cheddar

.Wedmore

Wells

'Meare

Polden Hills

Gla~tonbury

Street ●

*Thus is the Cauldron created, a natural
container of the energy of rebirth.*

Norse traditions. In the Celtic myths it is a single cauldron of regeneration guarded by three wise women. The most well- known image of Cernunnos is one that decorates the second century A.D. Gundestrap cauldron. The Cauldron of Avalon contains the energy of that heritage and carries the power of all that symbology. This adds strength to magic performed here, as it is an accessible link to the Otherworld.

This land within the cauldron consists of peat and you can stand on areas of it and feel the land literally quiver as traffic passes. The Cauldron is naturally a wet land, a flooded landscape but like any container, it can be emptied. Although the landscape may seem to be very natural water levels are managed and controlled.

In modern times the Cauldron, these levels, is kept drained by a series of pumping stations and sluices on channels, rhynes and redirected rivers that crisscross within it. (see Map Two). The movement of the water within the land impacts on the feel of it, on the manner in which the energy flows through it. I have stood and watched the water flow backwards; the tides were high, the sluice gates closed and a backlog of water building. The feel of this was incredibly strange, and there was a definite element of release once the tides changed and the flow out to sea reinstated

Back in 1791 the area of the Cauldron was described by John Collinson as that vast wild of moors or meres… formerly overflown by the sea.
At times it is possible to catch glimpses of what the Cauldron was like when it was a flooded land. In

Map Two
Some of the waterways within the
Cauldron ~ old and new.

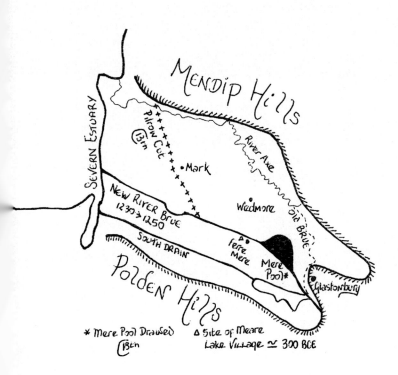

* Mere Pool Drained
  1810

△ Site of Meare
  Lake Village ≃ 300 BCE

autumn when the mists rise you can stand on the edges, on the Mendips or the Polden hills, or on the Glastonbury Tor and see the Cauldron of Avalon filled with mist and only the mounds of higher land projecting up through it like islands within a sea. Meare Pool which once used to keep Glastonbury Abbey supplied with fish only appears visible now in times of flood. Water is ever present here, and as such all of its powers influence: nurturing, growth, transition and emotions. This mixes with the symbology of the cauldron and creates a sacred and magical landscape full of the powers of transformation.

Droves are the green pathways that run in straight lines within this landscape; some of the fields that they outline are dug out peat works, many now flooded and transformed once more into areas rich with birdlife. The crossroads created by the droves or the routes of ancient pathways such as the Sweet Track of Neolithic times, hold a pulse of energy that sits only just below the surface of their physical reality.

As I walk through this landscape down the green droves breathing in the rich scent of meadow sweet, through damp woodland or alongside swaying reed mace, it all seems a positive illustration of the circle of transformation, of life, death and rebirth.

ဆ ★ α

There is an ecstasy to be experienced by breaking
down the psychological separation of oneself from
this land and truly connecting with its spirit.
Become one with the land that surrounds you, that
supports you, and it will share its magic with you.

When you look at the land that has become familiar to
you it is possible to see it with your intuition as well
as with your eyes, you can *Be* in that place both
inwardly and outwardly

We are of this Earth.
Our bodies are made from it:
We are born, grow, die, decay and transform to begin
again.
The pull of the rhythms of the Earth are present
within us if we are open to them:
Day and night
The changing seasons
The tides and the cycles of the Moon
Feel them
We are full of the wild
We are the Earth
and

This is a sacred landscape.

A Short *Bibliography* of books
recently revisited ...

Yvonne Aburrow   ~ Auguries & Omens, The Magical Lore of Birds ~ Capall Bann, 1994.

Paul Beyerl   ~ Herbal Magick ~ Pheonix Publishing 1998.

S. Buxton   ~ Shamanic Way of the Bee ~ Destiny Books, 2006.

J.Collinson   ~ The History and Antiquities of Somerset, 1791.

English Nature   ~ Somerset Levels and Moors Natural Area. A Nature Conservation Profile 1997.

K.Fletcher   ~ Somerset Levels & Moors, 1991.

R.Gibbs   ~ The Legendary XII Hides of Glastonbury ~ Llanerch Enterprises, 1988.

R.Graves   ~ The White Goddess ~ Faber & Faber, 1975.

G. Kindred   ~ Earths Cycle of Celebrations ~ G. Kindred, 1991.

K. Naddair   ~ Keltic Bird Law & Shamanism ~Keltia Publications, 1987.

J.D.Palmer   ~ Animal Wisdom ~ Element, 2002.

R. Ryall   ~ West Country Wicca ~ Pheonix Publishing Inc., 1989.

Barbara Walker   ~ Women's Dictionary of Sacred Objects & Symbols ~ Harper & Row, 1988.

C.L.Zalewski   ~Herbs in Magic & Alchemy ~ Prism Unity, 1990.

Acknowledgements and thanks are also due for the wisdom of friends and fellow witches shared throughout the past decades of Hedgewitchery

Thank you.

Sylvan Somethings C/o Silvasix@yahoo.com